Spark Joy:

An Illustrated Master Class on the Art of Organizing

|

Summary & Highlights

Authored By

Summary Reads

FREE GIFT SPECIAL REPORT

The Tidiest and Messiest Places on Earth

Learn about the Tidiest and Messiest Places on Earth! This report is a great supplement to this summary that is all about the virtues of being tidy.

As our **free gift** for being a **SUMMARY READS enthusiast** we are happy to give you a special report about the **3 Most Messy** and the **3 Most Tidy** places on Earth.

Learn about everything from **Garbage Island** to Computer-Chip **Clean Rooms** (and, of course, everything in between).

Get your **free copy** at:

http://sixfigureteen.com/messy

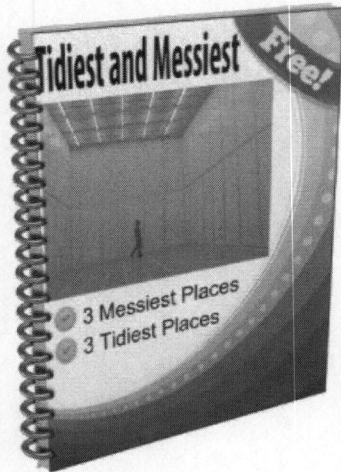

ISBN-10: 1523334355
ISBN-13: 978-1523334353

DISCLAIMERS

- Absolutely nothing in this volume is meant to constitute legal, financial, or medical advice nor are the opinions presented to be considered expert opinions.
- This volume is **NOT** meant to be a replacement for the original book, we believe our summation, key quotes and highlight analysis will increase interest in the complete book and not detract from it.
- In this volume, each particular detail is presented to the best of our knowledge and understanding of the recent book about tidying up. If you think any of our analysis or summation is inaccurate **please email us** and we will correct it and publish an updated edition after verifying (levelproperty@gmail.com).
- <u>Most importantly</u>: absolutely no portion of this summation volume was written in a Starbucks.

CONTENTS

SPARK JOY – *SINGLE PAGE SUMMARY*

Spark Joy is a book that breaks down the massive difference between cleaning and tidying. To tidy is to rid yourself of any objects that do not spark joy.

Clothing, kitchen supplies, cords, and any other item in your home must be sorted through to find the joyful and useful. This will help alleviate many tensions in your life and make your home, your dream home.

Many people spend their lives cleaning up because they do not know how to tidy and discard unneeded or unwanted objects.

Marie Kondo challenges the precepts of clutter and forces the reader to dig deep in deciding the actual need of an object.

After you put the principles of this book into your daily life you will find yourself in a clutter and stress-free world.

<u>NOTE</u>: we have included **some of our OWN illustrations** that visually show some of the concepts in the original text and drawings for your convenience and enjoyment (but the drawings themselves **are originals** – so please don't send us any nasty cease and desist letters!)

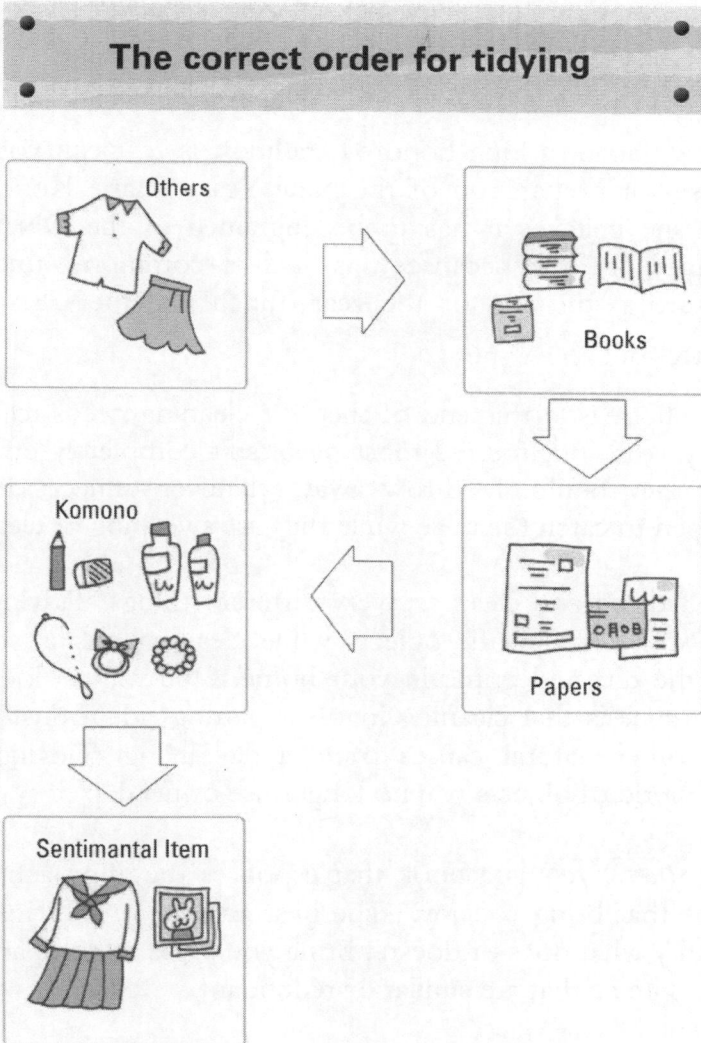

The correct order for tidying

Others

Books

Komono

Papers

Sentimantal Item

Figure 1: There's an Order to Tidying Up

CHAPTER 1: DIALING IN YOUR SENSITIVITY ABOUT JOY
(SUMMARY, HIGHLIGHTS & BEST QUOTES)

In Japan, a long honored tradition is to clean your entire house for preparation of the New Year. Marie Kondo states that she believes it has to be engrained in the DNA of the Japanese people because it is such a commonly understood venture at the end of the year, much like the USA's spring cleaning.

The reason this end of the year cleaning needs to be done every year and, for the most part, isn't completely effective is that they randomly throw away whatever unnecessary items happen to catch their eye while they are sweeping or cleaning.

Tidying and clean are very different things. Tidying means you work on specific objects while cleaning means you clean out the dirt and grime in your home. One way to look at the difference is that cleaning involves getting rid of dust and dirt and other natural causes of everyday living. Tidying means getting rid of objects you no longer use or need.

Spark Joy is a book that espouses the approach to keep items that bring you joy. The best and most effective way to identify what does or doesn't bring you joy is to compare it with others items that are similar or redundant.

Kondo encourages the reader to work on keeping the top three of each category. In looking at your favorite dresses, pick the three that give you the most joy. Sure you might need to keep others, for a job, warmth, or other task, but if you start with the idea of creating a Top 3 List it will help you keep your tasks

This whole process starts with clothing. Kondo suggests starting with tops. Tops are worn closest to your heart and are the easiest, in her estimation, to discover if its worn with joy or not. She says to try and touch it, hug it, press it against your heart and gauge your reaction.

Best Quote?

"I really tidied up at the end of the year, but I didn't manage to finish by New Year's."

"Tidying deals with objects; cleaning deals with dirt."

"Tidying up means confronting yourself."

"Cleaning means confronting nature..."

"Tidying orders the mind while cleaning purifies it."

"Does it spark joy when you touch it?"

"If it really doesn't spark joy, go ahead and discard it."

YOU DECIDE: @SummaryReads

Figure 2: Tidy Up Before Moving

CHAPTER 2: FILLING UP YOUR HOME WITH JOY
(SUMMARY, HIGHLIGHTS & BEST QUOTES)

In the race to tidy one's house it is imperative to concentrate solely on discarding first. Never try and organize as you go. Discard first and organize later. In the discarding phase please understand that the discarding isn't the end game. Many will try this method and give up because it gets depressing. The better parts are still to come.

Tidying gives you the chance to open up ideas and lifestyle looks that never seemed possible before. Don't curb your ideas or settle for something you mostly like. Dream big and work to create a home environment that is perfect for you.

One major no-no during the discard phase is keeping a box of maybes. Some designers suggest having a box of undecided things that you keep and if you do not use them in three months then commence with the discarding.

This works in principle but not in reality. What Kondo realized is that she would hate seeing that box and feel guilty over the items she was thinking about discarding. She found herself using items she didn't like or need just because she was consumed by guilt.

She would walk by the box and think about how the items in there were patiently awaiting their judgment.

When it comes to attraction there are three common elements:

- Innate attraction
  - Actual beauty of an object
- Acquired attraction
  - Amount of love poured into it
- Experiential value
  - Amount of history or significance it has accrued

Once you finish up the discarding and tidying steps you may discover that you don't feel completed.

This is, often, happening because of a lack of color in the home. It is incredibly important to keep a home full of things you love rather than focus on keeping nothing.

Bottom line is if it makes you happy, keep it and do not worry about any other outside judgment. In fact if you love it and it isn't practical there are four things you can do to properly display these items:

1. Place it on something
   a. In a bowl

      b. In a vase

      c. In a plate

  2. Hang it

      a. On a hanger for you to see

  3. Pin or Paste it up

      a. Make a corkboard of memories you want to keep

      b. Scrapbook

  4. Wrap it on or around something

      a. Use loved fabric to cover wires or other unsightly things

Best Quote?

"Imagine your perfect lifestyle from a single photograph."

"The act of discarding things on its own will never bring joy to your life."

"Judgment day is coming soon."

"If you just can't bring yourself to discard something, then keep it without and guilt."

"There are only two choices: keep it or chuck it. And if you're going to keep it, make sure to take care of it."

YOU DECIDE: @SummaryReads:

Lots of Ways to Spark Up Your Storage

Figure 3: Sparking up Storage

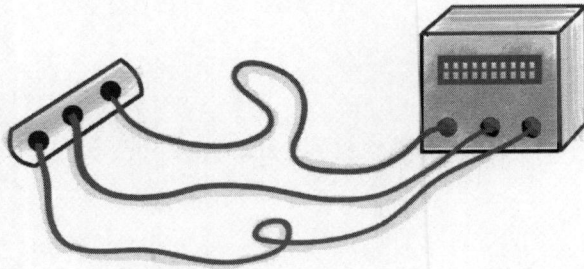

Wrap Things

Figure 4: Wrapper's Delight

CHAPTER 3: ALL YOU NEED TO KNOW ABOUT JOYFULLY STORING
(SUMMARY, HIGHLIGHTS & BEST QUOTES)

During the tidying process, storage is very temporary. As you tidy it is only natural for the room or house to get messy. In a later stage, the komono category, things will get very messy since it covers a large spectrum of items.

One way to help with the storage process is to store by material. As you store keep like materialized things together, such as keep plastic objects together and clothing together. This is not an exhaustive answer since there are some objects that are made of multiple materials, but keeping this idea in mind can help relieve the tension you may have in storing things properly.

When filling drawers for storage, remember to completely utilize the drawer. Do not let it sit at 70% full and do not fill it to overflowing. Keep it at a solid, but full, range.

In storage there are **four principles** that work with almost any item:

1. Fold it
2. Stand it upright
3. Store in one spot
4. Divide storage space into square compartments

Follow this basic folding method:

1. Fold both edges of the body of the garment toward the center to form a rectangle
2. Fold the rectangle in half lengthwise
3. Fold this in half or thirds

Basic Folding Method

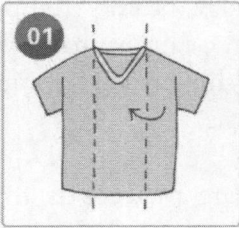

01

Fold one Side
of the garment
acrose the
center

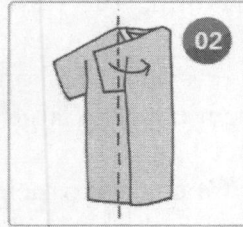

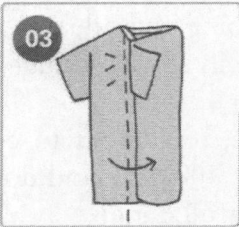

02

03

Fold the
oppsite side
the same
way

Stop a little
before edge

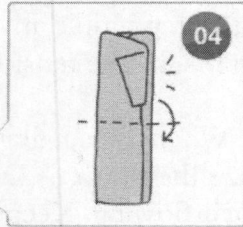

04

05

Leave a bit
of a gap!

Basic folding
method for
clothes to
stand upright

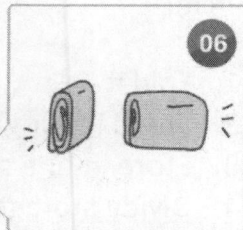

06

Best Quote?

"My three main material categories are cloth, paper, and electric."

"It's the moment, when, after discarding everything but the things you love, you know that you have all you need to feel content."

"The rule of thumb for storage is 90 percent."

YOU DECIDE: **@SummaryReads**

CHAPTER 4: TIDY UP CLOTHES
(SUMMARY, HIGHLIGHTS & BEST SIZZLE/STEAK QUOTES)

Your tidying campaign, as stated earlier, starts with clothing. Gather every item you own in your house and place in one location. Make sure everything you own is there before you start tidying.

HOW TO FOLD SHIRTS

Long sleeved shirts

For long sleeved shirts fold the sleeves toward the center to make a rectangle and do not let the sleeves overlap each other, this creates a bulge. After this fold in thirds until it matches the height of the storage space, and then stand it up.

Odd Shaped Shirts

To fold odd shaped tops you start by folding the sleeves into a rectangle and then fold like a normal long sleeved shirt.

Camisoles

Fold one side to the center and then do the same to the other. Fold down into a half, with the straps, and then take the bottom and pull it over the top half.

Parkas

Fold just like a long sleeved shirt leaving the hood exposed. As the folding is finishing fold the hood into the body of the parka.

Thick Clothes

Fold a thick sweater or other bulky clothing by placing them into an airtight bag and press the air out of it.

HOW TO FOLD PANTS

Place the legs together and then fold the seat part that sticks out from the legs to make it even with the legs. Fold the legs to the bottom of the waist band. Then fold into thirds.

HOW TO FOLD SHORTS

Match the legs and the extra seat like jeans. Fold in half.

HOW TO FOLD DRESSES

Match the sleeves and fold in thirds similar to a long sleeved shirt. Make sure the bottom part of the dress folds into the main body of the fold and fold until desired length.

You can tidy your closet by storing your hung clothes from tallest to shortest. This creates a very clean look.

Best Quote?

"That's quite a unique way of folding, isn't it?"

CHAPTER 5: TIDY UP BOOKS
(SUMMARY, HIGHLIGHTS & BEST QUOTES)

Tidying books, at first glance, seems to be a massive waste of effort. Contrary to that belief is the idea that tidying up books is an excellent way to increase sensitivity to joy.

The most common reason people don't want to get rid of books is that they may want to read it again. If the book doesn't spark joy in you now, it will not spark it in the future.

MAGAZINE AND COFFEE-TABLE BOOKS

Keep the magazines and pictures books that you would put into your "hall of fame" but discard outdated ones that cause no joy. If a magazine subscription you have tends to pile up, set a max amount allowed in your home before discarding.

To store books attractively make sure to keep them in the same category and never stack them in a pile, always stand them up.

Best Quote?

"As you continue tidying, you will hone your sensitivity to joy."

YOU DECIDE: @SummaryReads

CHAPTER 6: TIDY UP PAPERS
(SUMMARY, HIGHLIGHTS & BEST QUOTES)

Paper is so small and unassuming that a single sheet, that seems harmless, becomes an overflowing mess of papers that is out of control. The only way to successfully discard the papers you need to discard is to start with the premise that they will all be thrown away.

Gather all the paper into one location and starts making the individual sheets prove they shouldn't be thrown away, rather than you proving why you want to keep it.

As you do this it is also prudent to make a pending box. This will normally be reserved for outstanding bills, letters to be sent off, and other items that will be handled in due time.

It is prudent to cast off course materials as well. Even if the materials were something you wanted to keep, throw them away, studies show this helps with the process of putting into practice what you have learned.

Credit card statements are, traditionally, something we hold on to. However, once you rectify your balance and pay your payment their usefulness is done. Discard all old credit card statements.

Warranties normally are kept long past their expiration date. Kondo suggests keeping them in one clear binder and routinely checking the binder for expired warranties. Also do not feel burdened to keep old manuals. These are rarely used and can be recycled.

Greeting cards should only be kept if they spark joy AFTER completing their job.

Best Quote?

"The basic rule for papers: Discard everything."

YOU DECIDE: **@SummaryReads**

CHAPTER 7: TIDY UP KOMONO
(SUMMARY, HIGHLIGHTS & BEST QUOTES)

Komono stands for the miscellaneous items and is the most difficult category to tidy because it has an overwhelming list of subcategories such as: stationary supplies, electrical cords, food, cleaning supplies, laundry items, etc.

Three basic steps for each subcategory of komono
1. Gather all items in that category in one place
2. Choose only those that spark joy
3. Store by category

When tidying CDs and DVDs the key is to keep those that induce joy. If a CD brings joy because it is an old mix tape from an ex-lover, thank it for its usefulness and throw it away. One key is to not stop and listen to a CD or watch DVD while tidying.

Split stationary supplies in to three categories: Equipment and paper related supplies, and letter-writing supplies.

Equipment is a thing that does not diminish in volume such as pens, scissors, and staplers. Discard any that do not spark joy, especially promotional items such as marketing pens.

Paper-related supplies are the other side of stationary, paper, notebooks, memo pads, and the like. Discard all that have finished their purpose and do not spark joy.

Letter-writing supplies are letter papers, envelopes, postcards, and the like.

Electrical Komono
- Cords
  - Discard all mystery cords
- Memory cards and batteries

Skincare products should be checked for freshness. Check if the samples or travel size you keep is something you actually use, if so keep it, if not discard it. Makeup is similar, you must check for freshness.

Relaxation goods are things such as aromatherapy candles, oils, and other items for relaxing and healing. Check and see if these items spark joy and discard any that don't or are old and past their useful life.

Check your medicine for expired pills or empty bottles. Many medicines last longer than they should in their respective areas because they expire and no one checks on it.

With sewing and sewing items discard what is unusable such as small amounts of fabric or left over buttons. If a sewing kit is never used, discard it.

Best Quote?

"Keep only those letter-writing supplies that inspire you to write."

YOU DECIDE: **@SummaryReads**

CHAPTER 8: TIDY UP SENTIMENTAL ITEMS
(SUMMARY, HIGHLIGHTS & BEST QUOTES)

The most important part of tidying this category is to believe in your own sense of joy.

Important points to remember:

- Don't send sentimental items to your parent's home
- If you cannot throw it away, keep it with confidence
- Make good use of the things that stay

Work hard to discard old school items such as report-cards and school uniforms.

Put the keepsakes of past lovers on hiatus and discard them. This will not only clear up space in your tidying venture, but also free up emotion for new lovers that may cross your path.

Family photographs are a very difficult group of sentimental items to tidy. Take time with your family to recall the fond memories each picture represents. Decide which to keep and which to discard together. This will probably be the last of your tidying responsibilities, but it may be the most cherished moments you have in your tidying journey.

Best Quote?

> *"Tidying sentimental items means putting the past in order."*

> *"I only finished tidying up my photographs very recently."*

YOU DECIDE: **@SummaryReads**

CHAPTER 9: A HOME SPARKING JOY
(SUMMARY, HIGHLIGHTS & BEST QUOTES)

The savvy tidier can instantly tell the state of someone's closets by the look of the entranceway. An entranceway that you cannot enter is the home of someone that desperately needs to tidy.

You can decorate the entranceway by keeping small things that appear in order. Keep all other decorations in other areas of the house.

The living room is supposed to provide a space to gather and enjoy each other's company. It is the room that should speak the most about your family.

You should keep your kitchen clean (there is a difference between clean and tidy). This is a non-negotiable.

In the office area clear it out by discarding all unnecessary papers. Arrange books and materials according to your own rules.

Make your bedroom an oasis to recharge. Keep the lighting soft and indirect and wash sheets and pillowcases frequently.

In the bathroom take out only what you need and put it up once finished. The ideal bathroom has a fresh and natural aroma.

Best Quote?

"You'll have to come in the back door, there's no room to get in here."

"Keep your entranceway as clear as possible."

"Always keep in mind that it's (The Living Room) the center of family life."

"Moisture and oil are the enemy."

YOU DECIDE: **@SummaryReads**

CHAPTER 10: THE CHANGE WHEN YOU'RE DONE
(SUMMARY, HIGHLIGHTS & BEST QUOTES)

Many of Kondo's clients had a new air of confidence around them. Many even exclaimed that their love life improved once they climbed the tidying mountain.

Tidying brings relationships into focus. A truly tidied home brings families less stress at the end of a long workday. Without having to clean up constantly gives you time to connect with those you love the most.

After tidying you will become keen to those that need to tidy. It is imperative not to force others to tidy. This is a process that requires personal dedication and cannot be coerced.

One major step in your tidying journey is learning to accept people that have differing values. Once you can accept that you have finished tidying.

Once tidying has taken place in your life you can now bestow some of the virtues to your kids. Teaching your kids how to fold is an important step to them not being cluttered.

Best Quote?

"What kind of room do you want?"

"No matter the direction of the outcome, it is clear that tidying can also help us set our love life in order."

YOU DECIDE: **@SummaryReads**

FURTHER READING

Are you ready to quickly absorb the main points and highlights of the next best seller? Check out the other great summaries from *Summary Reads*:

■ Karl Rove's latest book, ***The Triumph of William McKinley: Why the Election of 1896 Still Matters*** is a great read, but it is a LONG book. We have already read it and summarized it for you so pick up a copy and enjoy:

http://amzn.com/B018Y0POJY

■ Brian Kilmeade's latest best-seller, ***Thomas Jefferson and the Tripoli Pirates,*** is a fascinating story about a forgotten war. Get the summary today:

http://amzn.com/B018B8FFWK

■ Crippled America is Trump's latest book and we have the top summary on the market:

http://amzn.com/B017QT0IMM

■ The over 900 page best-seller ***Destiny and Power*** is a great book but not everyone has the time for the whole book. Check out our summary and save hours: http://amzn.com/B019D70GI6

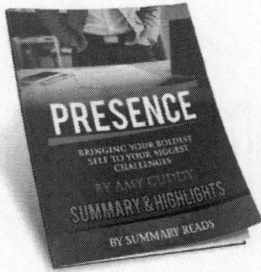

IF YOU LIKED this summary then you will **LOVE** our summary of **"Presence**: Bringing Your **Boldest Self** to Your Biggest Challenges" by **Amy Cuddy**…

Learn how **small changes** in your daily habits can have HUGE **positive effects** on your life!
http://amzn.com/B01A14U1W6

Last but **DEFINITELY NOT LEAST** is our best-seller summary of Mary Beard's *SPQR: A History of Ancient Rome.*

Get your copy today:
http://amzn.com/B018MANYA2

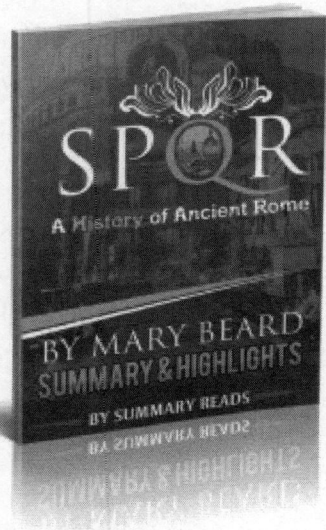

FREE GIFT SPECIAL REPORT
The Tidiest and Messiest Places on Earth

Learn about the Tidiest and Messiest Places on Earth! This report is a great supplement to this summary that is all about the virtues of being tidy.

As our **free gift** for being a **SUMMARY READS enthusiast** we are happy to give you a special report about the **3 Most Messy** and the **3 Most Tidy** places on Earth.

Learn about everything from **Garbage Island** to Computer-Chip **Clean Rooms** (and, of course, everything in between).

Get your **free copy** at:

http://sixfigureteen.com/messy

15313540R00022

Printed in Great Britain
by Amazon